The Bible Study Guide

Know Your Bible Inside and Out

Joel Graham

D1411695

CONTENTS

INTRODUCTION

Thank you for buying this book. It is my hope that through the information that you will find in this book that you will better be able to understand what the author of each of the books was trying to teach the people at the time and in doing so I hope that you are better able to apply these teachings to your own life.
We are going to cover each chapter of the Bible one at a time and learn about the author, the time that the book was written and why the book was written after this, I am going to provide you with a summary of the entire book as well as a few notable verses.

THANK YOU FOR BUYING THIS PINNACLE PUBLISHERS BOOK!

Join our mailing list and get updates on new releases, deals, bonus content and other great books from Pinnacle Publishers. We also give away a new eBook every week completely free!

Scan the Above QR Code to Sign Up

Or visit us online to sign up at
www.pinnaclepublish.com/newsletter

CHAPTER 1: GENESIS

The book of Genesis was written by Moses about 4000 BC. Genesis describes the creation of the Earth as well as the creation of the first man and woman, Adam and Eve. We learn about the first sin and what got the first people thrown out of the garden of Eden.

Later we learn the story of Cain and Abel, the sons of Adam and Eve. Upon offering their sacrifices to God, Cain became jealous because God accepted Cain's offering but not his. His anger was so strong that he committed the first murder and was sent away from his family.

We learn about the descendants of Adam coming upon a man named Noah. It is during his time that God decides to destroy the entire earth because it was full of evil. The angels had come down, falling in love with the women of the earth and their offspring, the Nephilim were quite evil, spilling blood wherever they went.

The people of the earth had forgotten their connection to God and had gone about doing whatever they wanted, worshiping false idols and living a sinful life. God saved Noah and flooded the entire earth only saving the family of Noah.

After 40 days and nights of rain, God provided the family with a rainbow as a sign of his covenant that he would never destroy the earth by water again.

The earth is repopulated; the tower of Babel is built and God confuses the language of man then scatters them over the face of the earth.

Abraham comes to the land of Canaan and we learn that because he and his wife Sara were unable to have a child, Sara allowed Abraham to take a slave girl into this tent, to create an offspring, even though God had promised the two of them that their offspring would be as the stars in the sky. Thus, the Islamite's were born. However, God keeps his promise, and Isaac is born.

Later we learn the story of Joseph and his coat of many colors. How a boy that was sold into slavery by his brothers would save the kingdom of Egypt as well as those same brothers from starvation when famine covered the lands. It is Joseph's story that begins to explain the great plan that God has for the Hebrew people.

Notable Verses:

Genesis 17:15-17King James Version (KJV)

15 And God said unto Abraham, As for Sarai thy wife, thou shalt not call her name Sarai, but Sarah shall her name be.

16 And I will bless her, and give thee a son also of her: yea, I will bless her, and she shall be a mother of nations; kings of people shall be of her.

17 Then Abraham fell upon his face, and laughed, and said in his heart, Shall a child be born unto him that is an hundred years old? and shall Sarah, that is ninety years old, bear?

CHAPTER 2: EXODUS

Exodus was written by Moses between the years of 1450 and 1410 BC. Moses, Pharaoh, Aaron, Miriam, Pharaoh's daughter, and Joshua are the key personalities in this book. The book was created to record the events that led up to the Hebrew people being delivered from slavery from the Egyptians, which are listed in chronological order.

It is in this chapter that we learn of the story of Moses, how Pharaoh had sent out an order to kill the first born of all the Hebrew people and how Moses's mother saved him by putting him in a basket and setting it upon the river. We learn that it was that Pharaoh's daughter that found him and raised him as the Prince of Egypt.

We also learn that it was Moses that would lead the Hebrew people to freedom. Once out of Egypt, God provided Moses with the Laws which were meant to provide guidelines to guide them in their relationship with Him.

Notable Verses:

Exodus 24: 15-18

15 And Moses went up into the mount, and a cloud covered the mount.

16 And the glory of the Lord abode upon mount Sinai, and the cloud covered it six days: and the seventh day he called unto Moses out of the midst of the cloud.

17 And the sight of the glory of the Lord was like devouring fire on the top of the mount in the eyes of the children of Israel.

18 And Moses went into the midst of the cloud, and gat him up into the mount: and Moses was in the mount forty days and forty nights.

CHAPTER 3: LEVITICUS

Leviticus was written by Moses between the years of 1445 and 1444 BC. The setting is at Mount Sinai, Moses, Aaron, Nadab, Ithamar and Abihu Eleazar are the key personalities.

This book was written to the Hebrew people so that they could understand their history as well as the Law that was provided to them by God and to help the Hebrew people understand God's holiness as well as his desire for the Hebrew people to act as a holy people.

In this book, God, through Moses instructs the Hebrew people and the Levitical priests on how they are to conduct ceremonies, offerings, and other celebrations.

It is in this chapter that God informs the Hebrew people what is unclean as well as the procedures that they need to follow when dealing with unclean things such as bodies of the dead, unclean animals, insects, food, diseases, birthing as well as cleaning. This was so that God's people could be protected from diseases and illnesses.

The Hebrew people are also given instruction concerning the Day of Atonement which was the one day each year that the High Priest would prepare himself to meet with God. This was when the High Priest would enter the Holy of Holies and offer a sacrifice to God to atone for the sins of the Hebrew people.

Notable Verses:

Leviticus 19: 5-8
5 And if ye offer a sacrifice of peace offerings unto the Lord, ye shall offer it at

your own will.

6 It shall be eaten the same day ye offer it, and on the morrow: and if ought remain until the third day, it shall be burnt in the fire.

7 And if it be eaten at all on the third day, it is abominable; it shall not be accepted.

8 Therefore every one that eateth it shall bear his iniquity, because he hath profaned the hallowed thing of the Lord: and that soul shall be cut off from among his people.

CHAPTER 4: NUMBERS

This book was written by Moses between the years of 1450 and 1410 BC. Moses, Aaron, Caleb, Korah, Joshua, Eleazar, and Balaam are the key personalities in this book. Numbers was written to tell the Hebrew people how to prepare themselves to enter the promised land. The Hebrew people however sinned and were punished for those sins. In this book, Moses also takes two censuses of the population thus the name of the book.

It begins by Moses taking the first census as the Hebrew people are preparing for their journey to the promised land. It is also during this time that the Hebrew people celebrate the second Passover which is one year after they were freed from the Egyptian people.

Next, the Hebrew people begin traveling in the wilderness toward the promised land and upon arriving 12 spies are sent into the land however only two of them return baring good news. This causes the Hebrew people to fear those that are living in the promised land and they began to rebel, not wanting to take the land. Because of this, God punished them, forcing them to wonder in the wilderness for 40 years until all that generation had died.

In the last chapters, the new generation again attempts to enter the promised land destroying two nations that try to stop them. However, they are seduced by Balaam and begin worshiping Baal. Because of this, 24,000 people die and the book ends with yet another census. Joshua assumes the role as the leader because Moses is not allowed to enter into the promised land because of his disobedience.

Notable Verses:

Numbers 23:19 NIV

God is not a human, that he should lie, not a human being, that he should change his mind. Does he speak and then not act? Does he promise and not fulfill?

CHAPTER 5: DEUTERONOMY

This book was written by Moses and was written between 1407 and 1406 BC. Joshua and Moses are the key personalities in this book. This book is a narrative history as well as the Law. Included in this book is a song that Moses wrote after commissioning Joshua. The song that Moses wrote talks about the history of the Hebrew people and the experiences that they had.

The purpose of this book was to remind the Hebrew people of what God had done for them as well as to remind them what God expected of each of them. The name Deuteronomy means Second Law and in this book, Moses is giving the Law to the Hebrew people for the second time.

The book begins by reviewing some of the history including the Exodus as well as the time that the Hebrew people had to spend wondering in the wilderness due to their disobedience. Moses urges the Hebrew people to follow the Laws given by God.

Later in the book, Moses goes over the Ten Commandments again, explaining the instructions that should be followed by God's chosen people. In the end of the chapter, we see that Moses hands over leadership of the Nation of Israel to Joshua and blesses the tribe. Finally, God allows Moses to see the promised land although is still cannot enter it afterward, Moses, on Mount Nebo, dies.

Notable Verses:

Deuteronomy 30:19 NIV

This day I call the heavens and the earth as witnesses against you that I have set before you life and death, blessings and curses. Now choose life, so that you and your children may live.

CHAPTER 6: JOSHUA

The book of Joshua was written by Joshua who was the Israelite leader between the years of 1405 and 1383 BC. The book focuses on Rahab, Eleazar, Joshua, Phinehas and Achan and it was written to reassure the Israelites that their God would reward them for being obedient to his commands and laws and it also records the conquest and the entrance into the Promised Land.

In the first four chapters of Joshua, we learn about the crossing of the Jordan river, and how the Israelites entered the Promised Land. We also learn of a woman named Rahab who was a prostitute, whom God has mercy on and whose line King David eventually comes from.

Next, we learn how Joshua followed God's commands and conquered the Promised Land as well as how the Israelites could conquer Jericho which at the time was a fortress. We learn how God was able to move and make the conquering of Jericho possible. Next, we learn about Ai which was the next town that the Israelites had to conquer although this one took two attempts due to sin that was going on in the camp. However, on the second attempt, God allowed the Israelites to conquer the town.

In the final chapters of the book, we learn how the land of Israel was to be divided among the tribes. Some of the larger cities are set aside for the Levitical priests because they were not to receive any of the land but to focus on their duties as priests. At the end of the book, Joshua dies but gives the Israelites a challenge that would last even until our time... "Choose you this day, whom will you serve...

as for me and my house, we will serve the Lord."

Notable Verses:

Joshua 1:11 KJV
Pass through the host, and command the people, saying, Prepare you victuals; for within three days, ye shall pass over this Jordan, to go in to possess the land, which the LORD your God giveth you to possess it.
Joshua 1:13
"Remember the command that Moses the servant of the LORD gave you after he said, 'The LORD your God will give you rest by giving you this land.'"

CHAPTER 7: JUDGES

The author of Judges is anonymous however, it is assumed that the prophet Samuel wrote it between 1086 and 1004 BC. It is a very interesting book that includes not only the narrative history but also riddles and poetry.

The key personalities in the book of Judges are Deborah, Samson, Delilah, Gideon, Ehud, Jephthah, Abimelech, and Othniel.

The purpose of the book of Judges is to teach the Israeli people that their God is faithful and true but that he will punish them for their sins if they are not devoted to him. In this book, we learn about the generations that come after the Promised Land was conquered as well as what happens when God's people are unfaithful to him.

Starting in the first chapter of Judges, we see that the Israelites have failed to keep the covenant that was made with God and that they never took complete control of the land that God promised to him.

From there, we see God raising up judges, hence the name of the book, who are to rescue the Israeli people. However, a cycle begins of sinning, being rescued, turning back to God then sinning again. Each rescue of the Israeli people only lasted for a short period of time because they continued turning their backs on God.

As the book goes on, the people of Israel, fall away from God and their morals seem to begin to die. By looking at the tribes of Benjamin and Dan, we learn how far they have turned from God. The tribe of Dan had turned almost completely to idol worship, to the point that those who participated in the idolatry defended their actions. It is because of the turning away from God that the tribe of Benjamin is almost completely wiped out leaving only 600 men after a violent civil war.

Notable Verses:

Judges 21:25 NIV

"In those days Israel had no king; everyone did as he saw fit"

Judges 6:8 KJV

That the LORD sent a prophet unto the children of Israel, which said unto them, Thus saith the LORD God of Israel, I brought you up from Egypt, and brought you forth out of the house of bondage...

Judges 16:17 KJV

That he told her all his heart, and said unto her, There hath not come a razor upon mine head; for I have been a Nazarite unto God from my mother's womb: if I be shaven, then my strength will go from me, and I shall become weak, and be like any other man.

CHAPTER 8: RUTH

This book is a love story but it is also about Genealogy. The book was written about the same time as Judges about 1046 to 1035 BC and while many people believe that it was written by Samuel, it is said that Samuel was probably not alive when the book was written.

The book contains the story of Boaz, Ruth, and Naomi. It was written as an example of the type of love that God wants us to have. It also shows us how things turn out when we obey God, versus what happens when he is not obeyed as in the book of Judges.

In the beginning of the book of Ruth, we find a woman named Ruth who although her husband and in-laws are all dead, remains loyal to Naomi, her mother-in-law. Naomi tells Ruth that she is going to return to Bethlehem, her homeland, alone. Ruth will not accept this insisting that she stay with Naomi and tells her "Where you go, I will go, where you lodge, I will lodge. Your people shall be my people and your God shall be my God..."

Later we find Ruth gleaning the fields of a man named Boaz who is a relative of Naomi's. Boaz has compassion for Ruth and not only follows the laws and allows Ruth to continue but he also orders that extra grain be left for her.

By the end of the book, Ruth and Boaz are married and have a son whose name is Obed. Obed would be the grandfather of King David and eventually, Christ would come from the same lineage.

Notable Verses:

Ruth 1:16 KJV

And Ruth said, Intreat me not to leave thee, or to return from following after thee: for whither thou goest, I will go; and where thou lodgest, I will lodge: thy people shall be my people, and thy God my God

Ruth 2:10 KJV

Then she fell on her face, and bowed herself to the ground, and said unto him, Why have I found grace in thine eyes, that thou shouldest take knowledge of me, seeing I am a stranger?

CHAPTER 9: 1 SAMUEL

The book of First Samuel is a narrative of what was happening at the time and it also includes much drama. The book was written by the last of the judges, named Samuel in around 930 BC. In this book, we learn about Samuel, Saul, Hannah, Eli, David and Jonathan. The book was written to show the Israeli people that while they had chosen a good king, they had abandoned their God.

As the book begins, we find that a woman, Hannah has given birth to a boy named Samuel and as a Nazirite, she dedicates him to God. Later, Samuel is brought to the tabernacle where he will live and spend his life serving God. It is during this time that the Philistines attack the Israelites and take the Ark of the Covenant, however, they quickly return it after they are struck with many plagues.

Next, we find that Israel has selected Saul to be king, believing that he will be great and while things go well at first, Saul begins to disobey God. Samuel tells Saul that God has rejected him as the King of Israel.

God has selected a young boy named David. Samuel anoints the young boy who several years later would stand up to the Philistine giant Goliath. David is able to kill the giant soldier with the protection of God by using only a slingshot and one stone, finally proclaiming victory over the Philistines and showing that he was a true leader. Saul is envious and jealous of David and hates him, he begins pursuing David because he is afraid that he will lose his place on the thrown.

David has the opportunity twice to kill the King but refuses to do so out of respect. Saul ends up taking his own life, later while in the middle of a battle that he was losing.

Notable Verses:

1 Samuel 16:1 KJV

And the LORD said unto Samuel, How long wilt thou mourn for Saul, seeing I have rejected him from reigning over Israel? fill thine horn with oil, and go, I will send thee to Jesse the Bethlehemite: for I have provided me a king among his sons.

1 Samuel 3:6 KJV

And the LORD called yet again, Samuel. And Samuel arose and went to Eli, and said, Here am I; for thou didst call me. And he answered, I called not, my son; lie down again.

CHAPTER 10: 2 SAMUEL

The second book of Samuel is the narration of David. We follow him as he becomes king and we learn of his reign. This books also includes two hymns in the last chapters. Samuel the prophet is the author and the book was written around 930 BC.

In this book, we learn about David, Bathsheba, Nathan, Joab, and Absalom. This book was written as a record of King David's reign as well as to demonstrate how to lead while submitting to God. In half of the book we learn about the King's successes then in the other half, we learn of his failures.

In the beginning of this book, David is crowned the King of Judah however, Israel, actually rejects God's decision and makes Ish-Bosheth, the son of Saul, their king. Later, Ish-Bosheth is executed and the northern tribes ask that King David rule over the entire nation. It is King David who establishes Jerusalem as the capital of Israel and the Ark of the Covenant is brought there.

In the later chapters of the book, we learn that King David has a sinful side and we see how the entire nation has to pay for his actions. David begins to lust after Bathsheba, then commits adultery with her which causes her to become pregnant.

David has her husband killed while on the battlefield, trying to repair the damage that he has done, however, Nathan, a prophet confronts David and David repents. Soon after David repents, the child died. Bathsheba and David have another son, Solomon who is to be the next king. Another son of the king, Absalom, pots against David and rebels, trying to take over Israel he is able to get the nation's approval. David must flee but he can eventually take his throne back and restore order to Israel. Absalom is killed.

Notable Verses:

2 Samuel 1:12 KJV

And they mourned, and wept, and fasted until even, for Saul, and for Jonathan his son, and for the people of the LORD, and for the house of Israel; because they were fallen by the sword.

2 Samuel 12:14

Howbeit, because by this deed thou hast given great occasion to the enemies of the LORD to blaspheme, the child also that is born unto thee shall surely die.

CHAPTER 11: 1 KINGS

The first book of Kings not only contains a narrative of what was going on but it also contains prophecy. The author of the book is anonymous however, many believe that the book may have been written by the Jeremiah, the prophet. The book was written between 560 and 538 BC.

In this book, we learn about David, Rehoboam, Elijah, Solomon, Jeroboam, Jezebel and Ahab. The purpose of this writing was to compare how the king of Israel ruled, depending on if they obeyed or disobeyed God.

In this book, we learn of the rule of King Solomon who would be the last king before the nation split. In chapter 8, we find a prayer to the Lord and later we learn what happens to the two kingdoms after they divide.

As the book begins we find that Solomon is the King after the death of his father David. David has told Solomon to walk in God's way and Solomon asks God to give him wisdom. God is pleased with what Solomon has asked for because he has not asked for riches, and gives him wisdom.

Solomon begins to build the temple which was a desire of his father and only seven years after he began building the Ark of the Covenant was brought into the temple.

Solomon, although blessed with wisdom by God, decides to do some very unwise things. He begins to worship the false gods of his wives and is overcome by his lust. Soon after Solomon dies.

After the death of Solomon, the nation begins to make the wrong choices and in 931 BC, splits. Rehoboam inherits the southern kingdom and begins increasing taxes. Jeroboam becomes the King of Israel, which includes 10 tribes. The tribes of Benjamin and Judah split from Israel and become Judah.

Elijah comes into the picture, warning Ahab, an evil king to turn from the worship of idols and return to the covenant.

Notable Verses:

1 Kings 17:1 KJV

And Elijah the Tishbite, who was of the inhabitants of Gilead, said unto Ahab, As the LORD God of Israel liveth, before whom I stand, there shall not be dew nor rain these years, but according to my word.

1 Kings 1:28 KJV

Then king David answered and said, Call me Bathsheba. And she came into the king's presence, and stood before the king.

CHAPTER 12: 2 KINGS

The second book of Kings discusses what is going on during that time as well as a prophecy about the division of Israel into two kingdoms. The author is unknown however, many believe that it was Jeremiah the prophet that wrote the book. It was written between 560 and 538 BC and in this book we learn about Nebuchadnezzar, Jezebel, Elijah, Elisha and many more.

The book was written to show how important it is for us to obey God as well as to show what happens to those who do not obey his commands. It is in this book that we learn of the many miracles that God performs through prophets that he has sent with messages. It is these prophets who bring hope to the chosen nation even though it is lost.

In the beginning of 2 Kings, we learn about those who are ruling the divided nation. Elijah hands his ministry over to Elisha who has followed Elijah as sort of an apprentice. Elijah is taken up in a whirlwind and Elisha asks God for a double portion of Elijah's spirit to which he is given. During Elisha's ministry, he performs double the amount of miracles that Elijah had.

We find that during the reign of Hoshea, the Assyrians invade Israel and take it into captivity because the Northern Kingdome had ignored the warning of judgment that was given to them by Hosea the prophet. After this, there is never a record of the 10 tribes of the Northern Kingdom returning to Israel.

The second part of the book we find that the Southern Kingdom or Judah is not doing any better than Israel. They are warned to turn from their wicked ways and to keep God's commandments but they do not listen.

Notable Verses:

2 Kings 2:11 KJV

And it came to pass, as they still went on, and talked, that, behold, there appeared a chariot of fire, and horses of fire, and parted them both asunder; and Elijah went up by a whirlwind into heaven.

2 Kings 9:10 KJV

And the dogs shall eat Jezebel in the portion of Jezreel, and there shall be none to bury her. And he opened the door, and fled.

CHAPTER 13: 1 CHRONICLES

The first book of Chronicles is not only glimpse into what was happening during the time of 1000 and 960 BC but it is a list of genealogies as well. It is believed that Ezra the prophet wrote it around 430 BC. The book talks about King David as well as Solomon.

There are some similarities with Second Samuel and the two books talk about some of the same events. Chronicles was written after the Exile in order to encourage those that had been in the captivity of the Babylonians but had come out. The book begins with the ancestry of the people, however, it is not in chronological order.

In the first nine chapters, we learn about the genealogy of the Israeli people beginning with Adam. The genealogy is listed for all 12 of the tribes of Israel as well as King David and the Priests. 4

Beginning in chapter 10, we find that the death of King Saul is reviewed as well as the reign of King David. It discusses the preparation that took place to build Solomon's temple. As the book ends, Solomon is the King of Israel.

Notable Verses:

1 Chronicles 15:16 KJV
And David spake to the chief of the Levites to appoint their brethren to be the singers with instruments of musick, psalteries and harps and cymbals, sounding, by lifting up the voice with joy.

1 Chronicles 3:4 KJV

These six were born unto him in Hebron; and there he reigned seven years and six months: and in Jerusalem he reigned thirty and three years.

CHAPTER 14: 2 CHRONICLES

The second book of Chronicles also appears to be written by Ezra the prophet about 430 BC and it talks about the events that occurred from the beginning of the reign of King Solomon in about 970 BC all the way up until the Babylonians took the Israelites captive in about 586 BC.

This book was written to show the blessings that a nation will receive if their king is righteous while also showing what happens when a nation has a sinful wicked king. This book is written from the viewpoint of the priest and it focuses on the correct way to worship God.

Beginning in chapter 1 until chapter 9 the book talks about the reign of Solomon, including his wisdom, and the construction of the temple.

The rest of the book talks about the events that occurred which split the nation in two. It talks about how Israel revolted against Rehoboam and how Jeroboam became the king. After this we see the focus shift to Judah. We also learn about the events that led up to the Babylonians taking Israel captive. However, in the final two chapters of the book, we find that God still has mercy on his people and the King of Persia, Cyprus allows the remnant to return to their land.

Notable Verses:

2 Chronicles 7:14 KJV
If my people, which are called by my name, shall humble themselves, and pray,

and seek my face, and turn from their wicked ways; then will I hear from heaven, and will forgive their sin, and will heal their land.

2 Chronicles 36:23

Thus saith Cyrus king of Persia, All the kingdoms of the earth hath the LORD God of heaven given me; and he hath charged me to build him an house in Jerusalem, which is in Judah. Who is there among you of all his people? The LORD his God be with him, and let him go up.

CHAPTER 15: EZRA

This book was written by Ezra around 440 BC and it is a record of the events that happened up until 450 BC. In this book, we learn about Haggai, Darius, Ezra and more.

The purpose of this book was to record the events that happened when the Israeli people returned to their land after being exiled by the Babylonians, which had lasted for 70 years. It also talks about the events that occurred as the temple was rebuilt in Jerusalem. This book shows that God is faithful and keeps his promises, because of this, the Jews are able to return to Jerusalem.

In the beginning of the book, we find that there is a small number of Jewish people in the city of Jerusalem but they begin to prepare themselves to build a new temple. They gather the materials that they will need and construction begins, however, it takes them a long time because they are surrounded by their enemies who are oppressing them and scaring them. Because of this, it takes them 20 years to complete construction on the new temple.

In chapters seven through 10 we see that a second group of Jews has returned to Israel, Ezra is one of them. He teaches the people of the law and has to address pagan women who have married into the Jewish people, and who have brought all of their false gods with them.

Notable Verses:

Ezra 7:10 KJV

For Ezra had prepared his heart to seek the law of the LORD, and to do it, and to teach in Israel statutes and judgments.

Ezra 10:11 KJV

Now, therefore, make confession unto the LORD God of your fathers, and do his pleasure: and separate yourselves from the people of the land, and from the strange wives.

CHAPTER 16: NEHEMIAH

This book was written by Nehemiah around 430 BC. IN this book, we learn about Ezra, Nehemiah, Tobiah, and Sanballat. This book is a record of the events that occurred as the Jews returned to Jerusalem up until 445 BC.

At this point, the Jews had a temple in Jerusalem however, they had no walls to protect them from being attacked. Under the leadership of Nehemiah, walls are built around Jerusalem in only a few weeks which caused the enemies of the Israeli people to lose confidence and leave the Israeli people alone.

In the beginning of the book, we see Nehemiah leading the people of Jerusalem in the construction of the walls.

Later, Israel begins to reestablish themselves as a nation after being held in captivity by the Babylonians. A renewal ceremony is led by Ezra. The Jewish people knew that they had to remember as well as obey the laws of their God and it is here that Nehemiah condemns mixed marriages, one of the reasons being that the children that were a result of these marriages were not being taught the Hebrew language.

Notable Verses:

Nehemiah 1:3 KJV
And they said unto me, The remnant that are left of the captivity there in the province are in great affliction and reproach: the wall of Jerusalem also is broken down, and the gates thereof are burned with fire

Nehemiah 9:10 KJV

And shewedst signs and wonders upon Pharaoh, and on all his servants, and on all the people of his land: for thou knewest that they dealt proudly against them. So didst thou get thee a name, as it is this day.

CHAPTER 17: ESTHER

It is believed that Mordecai, the cousin of Esther as well as the guardian wrote the book of Esther around 470 BC. In this book, we learn about Esther, Haman, Xerxes and Mordecai.

The purpose of this writing was to demonstrate that God is in control over all circumstances as well as show his love. It is the story of the Jews who stayed in Persia after they had been released.

In the beginning of the book, we find that Esther has become the queen of Persia because the king of Persia loved her more than any other woman and she had found favor with him.

Next, we find that Mordecai, Esther's cousin would refuse to bow down to Haman. This infuriates Haman and he vows to destroy all of the Jews left in Persia. Mordecai learns of Harman's plans and tells Esther.

It is Esther who takes matters into her own hands, asking the King to protect all of her people from Haman's plan. Filled with anger, the King has Haman hung in the very gallows that he had created to kill all of the Jews in Persia. Esther was able to save the Jewish people.

Notable Verses:

Esther 4:14 KJV
For if thou altogether holdest thy peace at this time, then shall there enlargement and deliverance arise to the Jews from another place; but thou and thy father's house shall be destroyed: and who knoweth whether thou art come to the

33

kingdom for such a time as this?

Esther 3:4 KJV

Now it came to pass, when they spake daily unto him, and he hearkened not unto them, that they told Haman, to see whether Mordecai's matters would stand: for he had told them that he was a Jew.

CHAPTER 18: JOB

It is unknown who wrote the book of Job, however, it is quite possible that Job wrote it himself. It is believed that the book of Job could be the oldest of all of the books that was written in the Bible, possibly dating back around 2100 BC.

In this book, we learn of a man named Job who loves God and whom God allows Satan himself to directly attack. Job is an example of the faithfulness we are all to have, even though he loses everything he still loves God and remains faithful.

In the beginning of the book, we find that Job is beloved by God but Satan is allowed to attack him, telling God that he will turn his back on him if he loses all that God has blessed him with. God tells Satan that he can test him but he cannot put his hand on Job. Job becomes sick and his wife tells him that he should curse God and die but Job refuses, remaining faithful and not blaming God.

Job's friends come to him, telling him that he must have sinned for God to allow him to suffer so. They give him terrible advice simply because they do not know God's plan.

Job loses his children his animals, and in the end, he is covered in sores, with nothing left, yet he never blames God for anything that has happened to him. Eventually, God speaks to Job and restores all that he has lost. God tells Job that humans do not know everything and explains to Job that people do not always understand what God is doing. God blesses Job with twice as much as he had before Satan afflicted him.

Notable Verses:

Job 1:6 KJV

Now there was a day when the sons of God came to present themselves before the LORD, and Satan came also among them.

Job 1:21 KJV

And said, Naked came I out of my mother's womb, and naked shall I return thither: the LORD gave, and the LORD hath taken away; blessed be the name of the LORD.

Job 1:10 KJV

Hast not thou made an hedge about him, and about his house, and about all that he hath on every side? thou hast blessed the work of his hands, and his substance is increased in the land.

CHAPTER 19: PSALMS

The book of Psalms includes poetry as well as songs and it was written by several people. King David wrote 73 of the Psalms, Asaph wrote 12 of them, Korah's sons wrote 9 of them, King Solomon wrote 3 of them and Moses wrote Psalms 90. 51 of the Psalms were written by anonymous authors and they were written over a period of 900 years, beginning in 1440 BC all the way through 586 BC.

The Psalms are directed at God and include praises, blessings, laments as well as thanksgivings. They are a way for us to express ourselves to Him and communicate with Him. The Psalms range from praising God to crying out in despair to him. They are found in the center of the Bible and one of the most common themes is praise.

Originally Psalms was divided into 5 books, book one was chapters 1 thru 41, book 2 was chapters 42 thru 72, book 3 was chapters 73 thru 89, book 4 was chapters 90 thru 106 and book five was chapters 107 thru 150.

The Psalms were written in order to help us know how to praise God, to teach us how God wants us to live and to find answers to the problems that we face in life.

Notable Verses:

Psalms 119:105 KJV
Thy word is a lamp unto my feet, and a light unto my path.

Psalms 127:3 KJV

Lo, children are an heritage of the LORD: and the fruit of the womb is his reward.

Psalms 111:10 KJV

The fear of the LORD is the beginning of wisdom: a good understanding have all they that do his commandments: his praise endureth forever.

CHAPTER 20: PROVERBS

Proverbs is made up of parables, poetry and as the name suggests... Proverbs. This book was written by Solomon, who is known as the wisest King to have ever ruled, however, some of the later chapters are written by Lemuel as well as Agur. The book was written between 970 and 930 BC. Solomon had asked God for the gift of wisdom and God had given him as he had asked.

The purpose of this writing is to teach God's people wisdom. The Proverbs are short but very clever explanations which are very easy to remember. These are things that are usually true, however, they may not always be. The Proverbs help us to deal with life, to have good judgment and to understand the difference between a wise man and a foolish one.

Solomon begins writing about wisdom for the young, providing parents with advice about raising their children. He teaches us to trust in the Lord and not to lean on our own understanding, just as Job was taught.

Beginning in chapter 10 and going until chapter 24, the Proverbs focus on wisdom that covers many topics and also spend time contrasting the difference between a righteous and a wicked man.

Later, the Proverbs focus on providing wisdom to leaders, providing warnings as to what will happen if they stray from God and instructing them on how to live a Godly life.

Notable Verses:

Proverbs 22:6 KJV

Train up a child in the way he should go: and when he is old, he will not depart from it.

Proverbs 31:10-17 KJV

10 Who can find a virtuous woman? for her price is far above rubies. 11 The heart of her husband doth safely trust in her, so that he shall have no need of spoil. 12 She will do him good and not evil all the days of her life. 13 She seeketh wool, and flax, and worketh willingly with her hands. 14 She is like the merchants' ships; she bringeth her food from afar. 15 She riseth also while it is yet night, and giveth meat to her household, and a portion to her maidens. 16 She considereth a field, and buyeth it: with the fruit of her hands she planteth a vineyard. 17 She girdeth her loins with strength, and strengtheneth her arms.

CHAPTER 21: ECCLESIASTES

Ecclesiastes is mostly an autobiography however it does also contain some Proverbs and sayings. The book was written by King Solomon about his life and it was written around 935 BC. Solomon had at this point become aware of his mistakes and he began to write them down. The purpose of this writing was to spare any future generations of the suffering that took place due to the mistakes that he had made.

It also appears that Solomon wanted this writing to teach wisdom to those that read it.

In chapters one and two, Solomon talks about the experiences that he had in his life and how he believed that none of it had any eternal meaning because it was all done in selfishness. Solomon talks about the meaning of his life and vanity.

Solomon, the man who God had granted wisdom tells us that even after all of the things that he has done, all of the things that he had experienced, there was no profit in any of it.

In chapters three to five, Solomon gives some explanations as well as observations, telling us that we come into this world with nothing and we will leave with nothing. He believes that all of our possessions, in the end, are useless.

In chapters six to eight, Solomon provides a bit of advice for those that wish to have a meaning full life. And then in chapters 9 through 12, he tells us that all of our deeds are done in vein if they are done without God.

Notable Verses:

Ecclesiastes 3:1 KJV
To everything, there is a season and a time to every purpose under the heaven.
Ecclesiastes 12:13 KJV
Let us hear the conclusion of the whole matter: Fear God, and keep his commandments: for this is the whole duty of man.

CHAPTER 22: SONG OF SONGS

The book of the Song of Solomon was written by Solomon sometime between 970 BC and 930 BC. It is a love poem about a groom who is in love with a bride.

This story is about the sanctity of marriage and that marriage is designed and blessed by God. It is also about the love that God has for his people. There is some sexual content in this book, however, it is a book that can teach us how much God loves us and how sacred marriage should be.

In the beginning of the book, Solomon writes about a courtship and an engagement of the Beloved who is believed to be Solomon and the Lover who is believed to be the Shulammite girl.

Next, we read of the marriage ceremony and the book concludes by talking about the relationship that a husband and wife have as well as how strong their love for one another is.

Notable Verses:

Song of Songs 2:3 KJV
As the apple tree among the trees of the wood so is my beloved among the sons. I sat down under his shadow with great delight, and his fruit was sweet to my taste.

Song of Songs 3:4 KJV
It was but a little that I passed from them, but I found him whom my soul loveth: I held him, and would not let him go, until I had brought him into my mother's house, and into the chamber of her that conceived me.

CHAPTER 23: ISAIAH

The book of Isaiah discusses the history of the Israeli people, contains a prophetic oracle as well as a parable in chapter five. The book was written by Isaiah who was a prophet around 700 BC, all except for chapters 40 through 66 which were written later in about 681 BC.

This is the first of the books that are described as the Major Prophets and they are called this because of the amount of writings that they authored, not because of the importance of the prophet or the prophecies.

In this book, we learn about Isaiah as well as Shearjashab and Maher-shalal-jash-baz, the sons of Isaiah.

The book of Isaiah contains prophecies pertaining to the birth of Christ as well as his reign on Earth. The purpose of this writing was to call Israel back to God and to declare that a Messiah was coming.

The book starts out by the sins of both the Northern and the Southern Kingdom's sins being pointed out by Isaiah. He tells them there punishment is coming not only upon them but as well as the nations around them. It is here that he states there is a Savior coming. In Chapter 7 verse 14 we read, *"Therefore the Lord Himself will give you a sign: Behold, a virgin will be with child and bear a son, and she will call His name Immanuel"* This prophecy was fulfilled in Matthew 1:22-24.

Later in the book, Isaiah discusses the return of the Jewish people to their land after being taken captive by the Babylonians. He again speaks of the coming Messiah.

The book finishes by Isaiah talking about the new Heaven and the new Earth, the reward that will be given to those who trusted and obeyed God. He also states that there will be a day of judgment for the evil.

Notable Verses:

Isaiah 9:6 KJV
For unto us a child is born, unto us a son is given: and the government shall be upon his shoulder: and his name shall be called Wonderful, Counsellor, The mighty God, The everlasting Father, The Prince of Peace.
Isaiah 7:14 KJV
Therefore the Lord himself shall give you a sign; Behold, a virgin shall conceive, and bear a son, and shall call his name Immanuel.
Isaiah 53:5 KJV
But he was wounded for our transgressions, he was bruised for our iniquities: the chastisement of our peace was upon him; and with his stripes we are healed.

CHAPTER 24: JEREMIAH

The book of Jeremiah was written by the prophet Jeremiah between 626 and 586 BC. The purpose of this writing was to warn the people of Judah of the judgment that was going to come up on them if they did not turn back to God.

In this book, Jeremiah points out the sins of the people and tries to get them to realize how serious these sins are. Jeremiah declares that there will be a new king and that a New Covenant will be made.

The book begins by God calling Jeremiah and Jeremiah condemning Judah of the sins that they have committed. It is obvious that he is angry because of their behavior.

As the book continues on, Jeremiah warns the people of Judah of the destruction that God is going to pour out upon them. We find that the people of Judah are worshiping false gods as well as burning sacrifices to them.

Jeremiah writes about a New Covenant that God will make with his people. The King, Zedekiah does not listen to Jeremiah's warnings but instead, throws Jeremiah in jail. Even so, Jeremiah warns Zedekiah that he is going to fall to the Babylonian King.

Next, we see the events unfold as Jerusalem falls, just as the prophets had proclaimed it would. The Babylonians exile both the Northern and the Southern Kingdoms.

Finally, in chapter 50 we find that God has promised to rescue the Israelites from the Babylonians.

Notable Verses:

Jeremiah 29:11 KJV

For I know the thoughts that I think toward you, saith the LORD, thoughts of peace, and not of evil, to give you an expected end.

Jeremiah 31:31 KJV

"The days are coming," declares the LORD, "when I will make a new covenant with the house of Israel and with the house of Judah."

CHAPTER 25: LAMENTATIONS

This book is filled with poems and songs that are sorrowful. As the name implies, the topic of this book is the expression of grief. This book was written by Jeremiah after the fall of Jerusalem about 586 BC. It is because of this book that Jeremiah is known as the weeping prophet.

Jeremiah, as well as other prophets, had predicted that these events would happen but Jeremiah actually watched the events unfold and in the writing of this book he reflects upon it.

The purpose of this book is, of course, to express the despair that he was experiencing but also to teach the Israeli people that if they disobeyed God, they would be punished.

As the book begins, we find that Jeremiah is mourning for Jerusalem as well as Judea, which lay in ruin. He goes on to talk about the anger of the Lord. In the third chapter of Jeremiah, he is expressing how troubled his spirit is, however, he reminds his readers that God is faithful and had promised to restore the people to their land.

In the fourth chapter, we find that during the siege, the people had suffered terribly. Starvation was so widespread that many had eaten their own children just to stay alive. We find that God has brought justice to the people who turned their backs on him.

Notable Verses:

Lamentations 1:1 KJV
How doth the city sit solitary, that was full of people! how is she become as a widow! she that was great among the nations, and princess among the provinces, how is she become tributary!

Lamentations 3:7 KJV
He hath hedged me about, that I cannot get out: he hath made my chain heavy.

CHAPTER 26: EZEKIEL

Ezekiel was written by the prophet Ezekiel around 571 BC and it was written as an announcement of the judgment that was to come upon Judah. This was to allow the people of Judah one more chance to repent and avoid the punishment that was to come.

The book also tells of the deliverance that the Israeli people would get from the Babylonians and spends a lot of time talking about the events that happened while the Israeli people where captive.

In the first three chapters, we find that Ezekiel has received a vision and he is sent to confront the people of Judah.

Beginning in chapter 4 Ezekiel delivers the message and tells several parables, teaching them that God would cleanse His nation.

Later, in chapter 25 we see that Ezekiel is condemning seven nations to judgment by God, Ammon, Moab, Edom, Philistia, Tyre, Sidon, and Egypt.

At the end of the book, a message of restoration is given, it is not only written to the people at the time of the writing but to the people who would be the future of Israel. It talks about the Messiah, the last Temple and the end of this age.

Notable Verses:

Ezekiel 18:20 KJV
The soul that sinneth, it shall die. The son shall not bear the iniquity of the father, neither shall the father bear the iniquity of the son: the righteousness of the righteous shall be upon him, and the wickedness of the wicked shall be upon him.

Ezekiel 20:21 KJV

Notwithstanding the children rebelled against me: they walked not in my statutes, neither kept my judgments to do them, which if a man do, he shall even live in them; they polluted my sabbaths: then I said, I would pour out my fury upon them, to accomplish my anger against them in the wilderness.

CHAPTER 27: DANIEL

The book of Daniel includes prophecies that pertain to the End of Times, as well as a narrative history. The book was written by Daniel who was a prophet about 530 BC and it includes records of the events that took place during the Babylonian captivity.

The book talks about visions of the apocalyptic time which were given to Daniel by God and which reveal the events that are to come which affect the future of every human.

In this book, we learn about Daniel, Shadrach, Meshach, Abednego, King Nebuchadnezzar, Darius, and Belshazzar.

The purpose of this writing was to not only provide us with an account of how God protected his people while they were being held captive but to also tell us of events that are yet to come.

The book starts out with Daniel talking about his live while in captivity. He describes how he was chosen to work for King Nebuchadnezzar and how he as well as his friends had to make tough decisions when it came to standing up for their God. They had to reject the king's food, pray to their God when it was illegal, and they refused to bow down to the idol which the King had made. It is here that Shadrach, Meshach, and Abednego are thrown into a fiery furnace but left unharmed.

Daniel also talks about interpreting the King's dreams on two separate occasions however, he never takes credit for the things that he has done, giving God all of the glory.

Later, we find that Daniel has received prophecies from God, he talks about the Messiah which is yet to come as well as the events that will happen at the end of time.

Notable Verses:

Daniel 9:27 KJV

And he shall confirm the covenant with many for one week: and in the midst of the week he shall cause the sacrifice and the oblation to cease, and for the overspreading of abominations, he shall make it desolate, even until the consummation, and that determined shall be poured upon the desolate.

Daniel 2:44 KJV

And in the days of these kings shall the God of heaven set up a kingdom, which shall never be destroyed: and the kingdom shall not be left to other people, but it shall break in pieces and consume all these kingdoms, and it shall stand for ever.

CHAPTER 28: HOSEA

Hosea is the first book in what is known as the Minor prophets. The Minor prophets are called this, not because the prophets nor their prophecies are less important but simply because the books that they wrote are short.

The book of Hosea was written by Hosea who was a prophet around 715 BC and it records the events that occurred during the years of 753 to 715 BC.

The purpose of this book was to show that although Israel had committed spiritual adultery, God still loved His people. Hosea was the prophet that brought the message of Got to the people of the Northern Kingdom after the divide.

It was during this time that the people of the Northern Kingdom were worshipping idols as well as oppressing the poor. God, in his grace, sent them the prophet, giving them one more chance to turn from their ways and back to him.

The book begins by Hosea being given instructions by God to marry an unfaithful woman. Hosea does as he is told but his wife, Gomer leaves him and goes to look for another man. Hosea is faithful to her and goes out to find her. He brings her back home.

Next, we find Hosea talking about how Israel, had been unfaithful to God just as his wife had to him but he tells the people of Israel that if they turn from their wickedness, God will forgive them.

Notable Verses:

Hosea 4:6 KJV

My people are destroyed for lack of knowledge: because thou hast rejected knowledge, I will also reject thee, that thou shalt be no priest to me: seeing thou hast forgotten the law of thy God, I will also forget thy children.

Hosea 2:3 KJV

Lest I strip her naked, and set her as in the day that she was born, and make her as a wilderness, and set her like a dry land, and slay her with thirst.

CHAPTER 29: JOEL

The book of Joel was written by Joel who was a prophet around 841 BC and 835 BC. The purpose of this writing was to prepare the Southern Kingdom for the judgment that they would face if they did not turn from their wicked ways. This takes place before the exile.

Joel tells the people of the Southern Kingdom of locust that cause damage to everything in their way and he tells the people that this is just the start of what they will face.

In chapter one, Joel talks about the locust, comparing them to the judgment that God will pour out on the people. In chapters two through three, he tells the people to repent and warns them that if they do not they are going to be punished. He explains to the people that if they turn from their ways, their land will be restored.

Notable Verses:

Joel 2:13 KJV
And rend your heart, and not your garments, and turn unto the LORD your God: for he is gracious and merciful, slow to anger, and of great kindness, and repenteth him of the evil.
Joel 3:7 KJV
Behold, I will raise them out of the place whither ye have sold them, and will return your recompence upon your own head.

CHAPTER 30: AMOS

The book of Amos was written by the prophet Amos some time before the exile. The book was written to the Northern Kingdom or Israel calling them to repent and to turn from their sins. However, the people of Israel rejected Amos and continued to disobey God.

The book begins by Amos describing Israel at the time, the people were tired of rebelling and although they were religious it was just superficial. Amos told the people that the nations of Damascus, Gaza, Tyre and Edom would be punished.

Amos tells the people that Israel is going to be destroyed and provides them with examples of the judgment that will come upon them. Finishing up this book, Amos provides the people with some hope, telling them that Israel will be restored.

Notable Verses:

Amos 8:11 KJV
Behold, the days come, saith the Lord GOD, that I will send a famine in the land, not a famine of bread, nor a thirst for water, but of hearing the words of the LORD.
Amos 9:11 KJV
In that day will I raise up the tabernacle of David that is fallen, and close up the breaches thereof; and I will raise up his ruins, and I will build it as in the days   of   old.

I NEED YOUR HELP

I really want to thank you again for reading this book. Hopefully you have liked it so far and have been receiving value from it. Lots of effort was put into making sure that it provides as much content as possible to you and that I cover as much as I can.

If you've found this book helpful, then I'd like to ask you a favor. Would you be kind enough to leave a review for it on Amazon? It would be greatly appreciated!

CHAPTER 31: OBADIAH

This book was written by the prophet Obadiah around 853 BC to 841 BC or between 605 and 586 BC, the dates are not for certain. The purpose of this writing is to teach people that God will judge all people who are against the Israelis. In this book, Edom is used as an example of how God will punish those that are against Israel.

Obadiah is the shortest book in the Old Testament, being only one chapter long, however, it is in this one chapter that we learn that Obadiah is a prophet of God and he tells of the judgment that will come upon Edom.

Edom had been against Israel since the ancients and if we look at the lineage of the nation we find that Edom actually comes from Esau who was Jacob's brother.

In the first nine verses, Obadiah tells us of the wicked Edomites, and how prideful they are. Then in the next five verses, we learn of all of the transgressions of the people of Edom. We learn that they should have acted like a brother to Israel because they were descended from brothers. Finally, we see that Israel will be victorious in the end, Edom was destroyed.

Notable Verses:

Obadiah 1:4 KJV
Though thou exalt thyself as the eagle, and though thou set thy nest among the stars, thence will I bring thee down, saith the LORD.

Obadiah 1:10 KJV

For thy violence against thy brother Jacob shame shall cover thee, and thou shalt be cut off forever.

CHAPTER 32: JONAH

The book of Jonah was written by the prophet Jonah around 785 BC and 760 BC before the Babylonians conquered Israel. In this book, we learn about Jonah as well as the people of Nineveh. The purpose of this writing is to show people that God is merciful and gracious.

We learn that although Nineveh was a wicked place and it should have been destroyed, God showed patience and sent Jonah to deliver a message to them.

The book begins by God telling Jonah to go to Nineveh, however, Jonah does not do what God tells him to do and instead, the boards a ship that is going to Tarshish. A great storm begins to brew and Jonah tells the sailors that it is God causing the storm because he disobeyed. Because of this, to save their life, the sailors throw Jonah overboard and he is swallowed up by a big fish.

Three days later, the fish spits Jonah out and Jonah went to Nineveh. He told the people that they had to turn from their wickedness and was surprised when the entire city repented. God teaches Jonah about his love however, Nineveh did not follow God for long and it was destroyed in 612 BC.

Notable Verses:

Jonah 1:5 KJV
Then the mariners were afraid, and cried every man unto his god, and cast forth the wares that were in the ship into the sea, to lighten it of them. But Jonah was gone down into the sides of the ship; and he lay, and was fast asleep.

Jonah 3:7 KJV

And he caused it to be proclaimed and published through Nineveh by the decree of the king and his nobles, saying, Let neither man nor beast, herd nor flock, taste any thing: let them not feed, nor drink water.

CHAPTER 33: MICAH

The book of Micah was written between 742 BC and 686 BC which is just before the Northern Kingdom would fall in 722 BC, and it was written by the prophet Micah.

The purpose of this writing was to warn the Northern and the Southern Kingdoms of the judgment that they would face if they did not turn away from their wickedness and back to God.

The book begins by giving specific judgments as to which the nation would face. Later in chapter five, we find that Micah prophecies that the birthplace of the Messiah will be in Bethlehem.

In the sixth and seventh chapter, Micah proclaims that God will save his people and that he will restore him. He states that God will not remain angry with them forever.

Notable Verses:

Micah 6:8 KJV
He hath shewed thee, O man, what is good; and what doth the LORD require of thee, but to do justly, and to love mercy, and to walk humbly with thy God?
Micah 5:2 KJV
But thou, Bethlehem Ephratah, though thou be little among the thousands of Judah, yet out of thee shall he come forth unto me that is to be ruler in Israel; whose goings forth have been from of old, from everlasting.

CHAPTER 34: NAHUM

Nahum the prophet wrote the book of Nahum between the years of 663 BC and 612 BC, which was just before Nineveh fell. Nahum was brought to Nineveh to warn them about the judgment that was to come from God if they did not turn from their wickedness, 120 years after Jonah had been there.

The purpose of this writing is to give Nineveh a final warning and to pronounce judgment upon the people. They had returned to their sinful ways after they had repented 120 years prior but this time, they would neglect to take the prophet of God seriously. In this book, the Assyrian empire is also addressed.

It would be no more than 50 years and Nineveh would no longer exist, being completely wiped off of the Earth.

In the beginning of this book, Nahum warns the people of Nineveh of the judgment that is to come upon them and then he addresses the Southern Kingdom, stating that there is hope for them.

Nahum tells Nineveh that it will be wiped from the Earth which we find is true because no remains of Nineveh were found until the 19th century.

Notable Verses:

Nahum 1:2 KJV
God is jealous, and the LORD revengeth; the LORD revengeth, and is furious; the LORD will take vengeance on his adversaries, and he reserveth wrath for his enemies.

Nahum 3:4 KJV

Because of the multitude of the whoredoms of the wellfavoured harlot, the mistress of witchcrafts, that selleth nations through her whoredoms, and families through her witchcrafts.

CHAPTER 35: HABAKKUK

Habakkuk wrote this book between the years of 612 BC and 589 BC which was just before Judah fell. In this book, we learn about Habakkuk and the Babylonian people.

Habakkuk is a very short book which is true for many of the other prophets' books but the information within this book was vital to God's people.

The purpose of this book was to announce the judgment that would come upon the people if they did not turn from their wickedness.

In the first two chapters, Habakkuk asks God some very difficult questions. He did not understand why evil was so prevalent. God answered him and told him that he was going to do amazing things that he would not even believe if he was told. He told Habakkuk that all of the nations surrounding Israel were going to fall and that the Babylonians would rule over all of the lands for a short time. He tells Habakkuk to be patient and to trust Him. In the third chapter, we find that Habakkuk is praising God for answering his question.

Notable Verses:

Habakkuk 1:3 KJV
Why dost thou shew me iniquity, and cause me to behold grievance? for spoiling and violence are before me: and there are that raise up strife and contention.

Habakkuk 3:4 KJV

And his brightness was as the light; he had horns coming out of his hand: and there was the hiding of his power.

CHAPTER 36: ZEPHANIAH

Zephaniah is a small book that was written in 630 BC, by Zephaniah. The purpose of this writing was to warn of the judgment that was coming as well as to encourage the people to repent.

During this time, before the exile, the Southern Kingdom had grown complacent with the wickedness in their lives. They had suffered under kings that were wicked and now they were to suffer again under God's judgment. However, Zephaniah also brought a message of hope to the people, a promise that while they would suffer judgment, Israel would be restored.

Chapters 1 and 2 take place 20 years before the Southern Kingdom is taken captive and yet it tells of what will happen to them if they do not turn back to God. Zephaniah also predicts the destruction of the city of Nineveh which is the capital of the Assyrian people.

In chapter 3 we learn how God gives us what we do not deserve, that being mercy. Zephaniah wrote that he hoped one day, a remnant of the people of Israel would be able to go back to Israel to fulfill what God had promised.

Notable Verses:

Zephaniah 3:17 KJV
The LORD thy God in the midst of thee is mighty; he will save, he will rejoice over thee with joy; he will rest in his love, he will joy over thee with singing.

Zephaniah 1:4 KJV

I will also stretch out mine hand upon Judah, and upon all the inhabitants of Jerusalem; and I will cut off the remnant of Baal from this place, and the name of the Chemarims with the priests.

CHAPTER 37: HAGGAI

This book was written by Haggai around 520 BC. It was written after the Jewish people returned to Israel from Babylon. The purpose of this writing was to encourage the completion of the construction of the temple. At this time, people had stopped construction because of the countries neighboring Israel. The Jews were afraid.

In the first chapter, God calls Haggai to deliver a message to his people. While they were sitting comfortable in their houses, the house of God was not finished. Haggai is able to get the Jews to resume construction on the temple and God blesses them for it. The temple was finished in 515 BC.

Notable Verses:

Haggai 1:4 KJV
Is it time for you, O ye, to dwell in your cieled houses, and this house lie waste?

Haggai 1:9 KJV
Ye looked for much, and, lo it came to little; and when ye brought it home, I did blow upon it. Why? saith the LORD of hosts. Because of mine house that is waste, and ye run every man unto his own house.

CHAPTER 38: ZECHARIAH

Zachariah is a book that was written after the return from captivity of the Jewish people and it was written by the prophet Zechariah. The first eight chapters were written between 520 BC and 518 BC, chapters 9 to 14 were written around 480 BC.

The purpose of this writing was to encourage the Jewish people who had returned to Jerusalem from their captivity. At this point, they had little faith in God and were lacking the motivation to build the temple. The people had to learn how to conform to God's law once again.

The book starts out by Zechariah recording a vision that he had and encouraging the people of Jerusalem to reinstate the religious laws that had been forgotten while they were in exile for 70 years. Zechariah provides hope to the people of Jerusalem and encourages them telling them that there is a Messiah who is coming and he will set up his throne and be their High Priest.

From chapter 9 through chapter 14, we find some passages that are a bit hard to understand, many of them are pertaining to the End of Times. It is also here that Zechariah writes down the judgments that will come against the enemies of Israel. The most important thing that we find in this section of the book is the prophecy of the coming Messiah who will be mounted on a donkey, betrayed, and crucified. At the end of the book, Zechariah writes about Jesus coming in the clouds as he descends from heaven.

Notable Verses:

Zechariah 9:9 KJV

Rejoice greatly, O daughter of Zion; shout, O daughter of Jerusalem: behold, thy King cometh unto thee: he is just, and having salvation; lowly, and riding upon an ass, and upon a colt the foal of an ass.

Zechariah 12:10 KJV

And I will pour upon the house of David, and upon the inhabitants of Jerusalem, the spirit of grace and of supplications: and they shall look upon me whom they have pierced, and they shall mourn for him, as one mourneth for his only son, and shall be in bitterness for him, as one that is in bitterness for his firstborn.

CHAPTER 39: MALACHI

This is the final book of the Old Testament and was written after the Jewish people returned to Jerusalem, after their exile. It was written by the prophet Malachi around 430 BC.

The purpose of this writing was to ensure that the Jewish people were following God and keeping him first in their lives.

In the first three chapters, Malachi talks about the sins of the Jewish people as well as the priests. He tells them that God is going to send them a messenger to prepare the way for his coming. Then he discusses tithes as well as offerings telling the people that if they do not give it to God, they are stealing from God.

In the fourth chapter, Malachi talks about 'the great and terrible day of the Lord', teaching the people of the judgment that is to come. However, he tells the people that those who follow the will of God will be spared from the judgment.

This book ends, quite different than the first book of the bible began, showing the people that they need a Savior because they have become separate from God.

Notable Verses:

Malachi 3:10 KJV
Bring ye all the tithes into the storehouse, that there may be meat in mine house, and prove me now herewith, saith the LORD of hosts, if I will not open you the windows of heaven, and pour you out a blessing, that there shall not be room enough to receive it.

Malachi 3:1 KJV

Behold, I will send my messenger, and he shall prepare the way before me: and the LORD, whom ye seek, shall suddenly come to his temple, even the messenger of the covenant, whom ye delight in: behold, he shall come, saith the LORD of hosts.

CHAPTER 40: MATTHEW

The book of Matthew is a Gospel of Jesus Christ, it was written by the Disciple of Jesus, Matthew around 48 AD and 50 AD. The word 'Kingdom' is used in this book 28 times.

In this book, we learn about Mary and Joseph, John the Baptist, Jesus, and his Twelve Disciples. We also learn about Pilate and even the Pharisees who are religious leaders of the Jewish people but who also try to stop Jesus from doing his work.

This is the first of the Gospels and it was written so that the readers would know that Jesus was the Messiah. It was also written in hopes of convincing the Jewish people that Jesus was the Messiah that they had been waiting on for so long, although to this day, they still wait.

The first four chapters of Matthew talk about the miracle that surrounded the birth of Jesus as well as his early life. This is what we have come to know as the "Christmas Story" but it is also here that we find the genealogy of Jesus being traced back to Abraham.

From chapter five to chapter twenty-five, we learn about Jesus's ministry and John the Baptist is introduced. We follow Jesus all the way up to the time that he is crucified. These chapters are very important for us to understand because it shows us that Jesus lived without sin while on this Earth. This is also where you will find the Sermon on the Mount, as well as many teachings of Jesus and the performance of miracles.

From chapter twenty-six to twenty-eight, we read about the death of Christ as well as the resurrection. These chapters of often referred to as the Good News of Jesus Christ. We learn how Jesus took all of the sin in the world upon himself and in doing so, became the perfect sacrifice, the final sacrifice. It is here that we see numerous prophecies in the Old Testament fulfilled, such as being crucified with two robbers and being betrayed for thirty pieces of silver.

Notable Verses:

Matthew 5:17 KJV
Think not that I am come to destroy the law, or the prophets: I am not come to destroy, but to fulfil.
Matthew 4:1 KJV
Then was Jesus led up of the spirit into the wilderness to be tempted of the devil.
Matthew 7:13 KJV
Enter ye in at the strait gate: for wide is the gate, and broad is the way, that leadeth to destruction, and many there be which go in thereat.

CHAPTER 41: MARK

Mark is the second Gospel of Jesus Christ and it contains a narrative of the life and ministry of Jesus. The words immediately is mentioned in the book of Mark 34 times and it is the shortest of the Gospels. The book of Mark was written by John Mark who was a missionary that had accompanied Paul and Barnabas as well as Peter while he was in Rome. The book was written around 64 AD.

The purpose of this writing was to show that Jesus was indeed the Son of God and the 16 chapters are divided into 2 parts. The first 8 chapters of Mark talk about when Jesus was traveling north, preaching the last 8 chapters talk about how he traveled south and to the cross.

In the first chapter of Mark, John the Baptist is introduced, Jesus is baptized in the Jordan River as well as tempted by Satan in the desert.

From chapters 2 through 10, we follow Jesus as he selects his 12 disciples, we see Jesus teaching multitudes, healing, and performing many miracles.

From chapter 11 on, we learn about the death and the resurrection, how Jesus was betrayed, put on trial, beaten and crucified all so that sinners might be saved. The final chapter of the book is about the resurrection, how Jesus's body appeared as well as the final ascension.

Notable Verses:

Mark 16:9 KJV
Now when Jesus was risen early the first day of the week, he appeared first to Mary Magdalene, out of whom he had cast seven devils.

Mark 10:45 KJV
For even the Son of man came not to be ministered unto, but to minister, and to give his life a ransom for many.

Mark 1:9 KJV
And it came to pass in those days, that Jesus came from Nazareth of Galilee, and was baptized of John in Jordan.

CHAPTER 42: LUKE

The book of Luke is the third of the Gospels of Jesus Christ. There are 18 parables found in this book which is more than any of the other gospels. It was written by Luke who was a doctor around 59 AD to 61 AD. Luke had accompanied Paul on many journeys. In the book of Luke, the words, 'Son of Man' are mentioned 80 times.

This writing was created so that we might know the truth of the life of Christ and understand that he was the Messiah.

In the first four chapters, we find that Luke tells us of the details that surrounded the birth of Christ and we learn how John the Baptist was sent to prepare a way for the Messiah. John the Baptist baptizes Jesus in the Jordan and Jesus begins his ministry.

In chapters five through twenty-one, we follow Jesus throughout his ministry as the hills the sick teaches and performs other miracles. Jesus also meets with different religious leaders who are trying to trick him so that they can have him killed.

From chapter twenty-two to the end of the book, we see that Judas has betrayed Jesus, which led to Jesus being convicted and sentenced to death by crucifixion. We also learn how just three days later Jesus rose from the dead.

Notable Verses:

Luke 4:18 KJV
The Spirit of the Lord is upon me because he hath anointed me to preach the gospel to the poor; he hath sent me to heal the brokenhearted, to preach deliverance

to the captives, and recovering of sight to the blind, to set at liberty them that are bruised...

Luke 9:23 KJV

And he said to them all, If any man will come after me, let him deny himself, and take up his cross daily, and follow me.

CHAPTER 43: JOHN

John is the fourth Gospel of Jesus Christ which contains the teachings of Jesus, sermons, and parables. This book was written by John the Disciple of Jesus about 85 AD to 95 AD.

This writing was created so that all would believe that Jesus was the Son of God and be saved. In this book, the word believe is mentioned 98 times and the word life is mentioned 36 times. This is because John wanted to get across to the readers that you have to believe if you are to have eternal life.

In the first chapter of John, we see John giving us proof that Jesus was not just a man, "In the beginning was the Word and the Word was God and the Word was with God..." John tells us that the Word has been made flesh and is living among the people. This is to show us that Jesus is not just a man but instead, God in the flesh.

From chapter two through chapter twelve, we learn of Jesus's ministry, how he met with Nicodemus and taught that no one could enter the kingdom of Heaven lest they be born again. Several times we see Jesus explaining that he is the only way to heaven.

From chapters thirteen to seventeen, we see Jesus, less than 24 hours before he would be crucified, taking part in the last supper, and discussing many important topics with his Disciples.

From chapter 18 to the end of this book, we learn of Jesus's betrayal, his death and how he appeared to Mary Magdalen as well as his disciples after he rose.

Notable Verses:

John 3:16 KJV

For God so loved the world, that he gave his only begotten Son, that whosoever believeth in him should not perish, but have everlasting life.

John 14:6 KJV

Jesus saith unto him, I am the way, the truth, and the life: no man cometh unto the Father, but by me.

CHAPTER 44: ACTS

The book of Acts was written by Luke, around 60 AD to 62 AD. The book is called Acts because it records the Acts of the Apostles. In this book, we learn of John, James, Paul, Peter, Timothy, Lydia, Stephen, Apollos and Silas.

This book was written as a way to spread the Gospel and it was to show the future church how they should behave. It is a record of the birth of the church and how the church transformed from being only for the Jewish to accepting the Gentile. This book shows us that Christianity has Jewish origins and that salvation was not just for the Jews but for the Gentiles as well.

In the first six chapters, we learn about the church as it was in its infancy. We learn about the Day of Pentecost and we see Peter giving a sermon to the Jewish people during the Feast of Weeks which resulted in 3000 finding salvation.

After this, the focus shifts and we see the Apostles are teaching others, besides the Jewish people, of Jesus. Stephen is stoned to death and we are introduced to Saul who would later become known as Paul. We learn how Saul persecuted Christians until one day while he was on his way to Damascus, he has a life-changing experience.

Beginning in verse 32 of chapter 9, we see that Peter begins to share the Gospel with the Gentiles, after having a revelation that Jesus did not only come to save the Jews. Saul, known by Paul at this point, has begun preaching the gospel as well and the word Christian is used for the first time in Antioch.

Next, we find that Paul and Barnabas are starting their journeys as missionaries to the Gentiles but are not allowed to enter Asia. Next, we learn of Lydia who was a woman that sold purple fabric. Lydia was the first to become a convert followed by the rest of her household.

In the end of the book, we find that Paul has been arrested and he has a difficult journey to Rome where he will be tried. Acts, however, ends before we find out what Caesar chooses to do with Paul.

Notable Verses:

Acts 1:8 KJV

But ye shall receive power, after that the Holy Ghost is come upon you: and ye shall be witnesses unto me both in Jerusalem, and in all Judaea, and in Samaria, and unto the uttermost part of the earth.

Acts 4:12 KJV

Neither is there salvation in any other: for there is none other name under heaven given among men, whereby we must be saved.

CHAPTER 45: ROMANS

The book of Romans is a letter that was written by Paul around 56 AD to 57 AD. In this book, we learn about Paul and Phoebe whose job it was to deliver Paul's letters. The letter is written to the believers of Rome, thus the name Romans.

Romans provides us with answers to some very important questions as well as discusses many other topics such as judgment, righteousness, and salvation to name a few.

Paul teaches through this letter that man cannot through his good deeds alone enter into the kingdom of Heaven but only by believing in Jesus as the Messiah would they be able to attain salvation.

He teaches us that no matter how many good deeds we do, we cannot create a relationship with God through these deeds, the only way that we are to have a relationship with God is through Jesus.

In the first eight chapters, we learn about the Christian faith, how salvation is a free gift from Jesus and how all men are sinners in the eyes of God.

In the next three chapters, we learn that we must confess with our mouths and believe in our hearts that Jesus is the Lord and that God raised him from the dead if we want to be saved. We are to put our faith in Jesus.

In the last chapters of the book, we learn how we are supposed to live. We learn that our bodies are to be the living and holy sacrifice and that we are not to conform to this world.

Notable Verses:

Romans 10:9 KJV

That if thou shalt confess with thy mouth the Lord Jesus, and shalt believe in thine heart that God hath raised him from the dead, thou shalt be saved.

Romans 6:23 KJV

For the wages of sin is death; but the gift of God is eternal life through Jesus Christ our Lord.

CHAPTER 46: 1 CORINTHIANS

This book is another letter from Paul and it was written around 56 AD. In this book, we learn more about Paul, Timothy and about Chloe's family. Paul wrote this letter to the Church in Corinth in order to address some of the division and immorality that had made its way into the church.

In the first four chapters, we find that Paul has been told of the problems in the church and begins to address them. He tells the church to consider their calling and tells them that God has chosen them.

In the next six chapters, we see Paul talking about all of the immorality that has entered the church which included believers filing lawsuits against other believers, sexual immorality and issues within marriages. Paul warns the people that they have been bought with a price and that they have to be careful how they live.

Next, Paul focuses on clearing up some confusion that was going on about worship and he corrects the doctrine of the church. Finally, Paul brings the attention of the church back to Jesus Christ and his resurrection telling them that this is the most important topic.

Notable Verses:

1 Corinthians 13:4-7 KJV
4 Charity suffereth long, and is kind; charity envieth not; charity vaunteth not itself, is not puffed up, 5 Doth not behave itself unseemly, seeketh not her own, is not easily provoked, thinketh no evil; 6 Rejoiceth not in iniquity, but rejoiceth in

the truth; 7 Beareth all things, believeth all things, hopeth all things, endureth all things.

CHAPTER 47: 2 CORINTHIANS

Second Corinthians is a letter that was written by Paul around 56 AD to the church in Corinth in order to teach the church about false teachers.

In the first seven chapters, we learn about the characteristics of the Apostles, Paul tells the church that his ministry was about preaching Jesus Christ, not about himself.

Next, Paul explains to the church that Christians are going to suffer but in comparison to spending eternity with Christ, the sufferings that we go through are nothing and he reminds them that it is only temporary.

In chapters eight and night, Paul tells the Corinthians that they should give offerings to those in Judea that believe as they had promised they would do.

In the next three chapters, we find Paul defending his ministry as he has been attacked, the Corinthians having questioned his authority. Paul tells them that if anyone teaches differently than Jesus, they are false teachers and their teachings should be rejected.

In the last chapters, we learn that Paul has had to deal with suffering just like the rest of us but when he had asked God to remove the suffering God told him, "My grace is sufficient for you..." Paul knew that God was in control of the things that he was going through and embraced the suffering. He understood that it was this suffering which ensured he remained dependent upon God.

Finally, Paul tells the church that if they want to see if they have faith in Jesus and are a true follower, that they must examine themselves with scripture.

Notable Verses:

2 Corinthians 5:17 KJV

Therefore if any man be in Christ, he is a new creature: old things are passed away; behold, all things are become new.

2 Corinthians 6:14 KJV

Be ye not unequally yoked together with unbelievers: for what fellowship hath righteousness with unrighteousness? and what communion hath light with darkness?

CHAPTER 48: GALATIANS

The book of Galatians is a letter from Paul which was written around 49 AD and it is believed that this could have been Paul's first letter.

In the first two chapters, we see that Paul testifies that he has received that Gospel message and he states that if anyone is teaching another message besides what he is teaching they should be rejected.

Paul states that Christ lives in him and empowers him to live as His instrument. In chapters three through five, we find that Paul is telling us that salvation is only through Christ and cannot be obtained any other way, not even through keeping the law.

He teaches us that no one can keep the law, it was impossible to do and still is, this is why there were sacrifices, however, Jesus was the final sacrifice. However, this does not mean that we do not have to strive to follow the law while following Jesus

In the final verses of the book, we learn about the fruits of the spirit. Paul tells us that while good works are not going to get us into heaven it should be the desire of every Christian to have good fruit, follow the law of God and live a righteous life.

Notable Verses:

Galatians 5:22 KJV
But the fruit of the Spirit is love, joy, peace, longsuffering, gentleness, goodness, faith...
Galatians 2:20 KJV
I am crucified with Christ: neverthless I live; yet not I, but Christ liveth in me:

and the life which I now live in the flesh I live by the faith of the Son of God, who loved me, and gave himself for me.

CHAPTER 49: EPHESIANS

The book of Ephesians is a letter that was written by Paul while he was in prison around 60 AD to 62 AD. This letter was written in order to encourage the believers to continue to follow Christ even though they were being persecuted.

In the first three chapters, we find Paul telling us how God has chosen us before he had even created the foundations of the world. He tells us that we are adopted into the family as sons and daughters of Christ. Paul continues all by talking about how grace is only obtained through faith and that no one can obtain salvation through good works.

In the next two chapters, we read that Paul is encouraging the believers and telling them that they should live as servants of Jesus. Paul teaches about how families should function, about marriage as well as how a husband should love their wives.

In the last chapter, Paul tells the believers that they have to put on the full armor of God if they are going to be prepared for spiritual battle.

Notable Verses:

Ephesians 2:8 KJV
For by grace are ye saved through faith; and that not of yourselves: it is the gift of God.

Ephesians 6:12 KJV

For we wrestle not against flesh and blood, but against principalities, against powers, against the rulers of the darkness of this world, against spiritual wickedness in high places.

CHAPTER 50: PHILIPPIANS

The book of Philippians is a letter that Paul wrote to the Philippians while he was in prison around 62 AD. He wrote the letter to show that he appreciated and loved the Philippians and wanted to encourage them as well.

In the first chapter of the book of Philippians, we find Paul writing about how he is suffering and that because of his imprisonment, the gospel was spread even further. He tells us that we are to surrender our lives to the service of Jesus and that in doing so we should expect to suffer.

In the second chapter, Paul talks about having the mind of Christ. Then, in chapter three he begins encouraging the church to continue and spread the Gospel. In Chapter four, Paul tells the church to rejoice in the Lord and finishes by telling them that they are blessed.

Notable Verses:

Philippians 4:6 KJV
Be careful for nothing; but in every thing by prayer and supplication with thanksgiving let your requests be made known unto God.
Philippians 3:20 KJV
For our conversation is in heaven; from whence also we look for the Saviour, the Lord Jesus Christ.

CHAPTER 51: COLOSSIANS

This book was a letter that was written by Paul while he was in prison around 60 AD and 62 AD and it was written to encourage the believers to continue to serve with passion. Paul was addressing the fact that the Judaic- Gnostic were trying to mix the Greek beliefs alongside of the Christian theology.

The Gnostic's taught that instead of having what they called god, create evil such as the devil, that there were lesser gods that were able to create which is where evil came from. The name of the lesser deity was Jehovah, God of Hebrews.

In the first two chapters, we see that Paul is sending his thanks to those who have been faithful in their belief. Although Paul had not established the Colossian Church and he had never visited the church, he sends them this letter because it is apparent to him that there are false teachers which are rejecting the fact that Jesus was the son of God.

Paul tells the people not to let anyone lead them astray from what they have been taught and to be careful of the trickery of men. Paul reassures the church that Christ was God in the flesh.

In the last two chapters, Paul tells the church that they should set their minds on the things that are above and focuses on teaching them how they should be living at home, how to take care of matters of the family and how to get along with other Christians. He tells them that they need to put aside the petty issues that they have allowed to become obstacles because it is these that slow down the spread of the gospel of Jesus.

Notable Verses:

Colossians 1:16 KJV

For by him were all things created, that are in heaven, and that are in earth, visible and invisible, whether they be thrones, or dominions, or principalities, or powers: all things were created by him, and for him.

Colossians 3:16 KJV

Let the word of Christ dwell in you richly in all wisdom; teaching and admonishing one another in psalms and hymns and spiritual songs, singing with grace in your hearts to the Lord.

CHAPTER 52: 1 THESSALONIANS

This book is a letter that was written by Paul around 52 AD and 54 AD and it is one of the first letters that he ever wrote. He wrote this letter to the church of Thessalonica in order to encourage them. In the letter, he focuses on the second coming of Jesus as well as, love, hope, and faith.

In the first three chapters, we see Paul commending the church for their faithfulness to God. Then in the last two chapters, Paul focuses on hope and love, encouraging the church to walk in love. Then he spends a little bit of time talking about the last days and how Jesus will come in the clouds during those days.

Notable Verses:

1 Thessalonians 4:13 KJV
But I would not have you to be ignorant, brethren, concerning them which are asleep, that ye sorrow not, even as others which have no hope.
1 Thessalonians 4:16 KJV
For the Lord himself shall descend from heaven with a shout, with the voice of the archangel, and with the trump of God: and the dead in Christ shall rise first...

CHAPTER 53: 2 THESSALONIANS

The second book of Thessalonians is a letter that was written to the church in Thessalonica around 52 AD and 54 AD. Paul wrote the second letter months after the wrote the first. In this, the second letter, he focuses on the coming of Christ because some people believed that Christ had already returned and he wanted to correct their beliefs.

In the first chapter, Paul focuses on the hope of Jesus returning, although the time that he would return would not be known. He tells the church that God will punish those that persecute the Christians in the last days.

In the next two chapters of the book, we see Paul speaking once again of the return of Jesus, giving the church signs that they should be looking for such as the antichrist and stating that all of the believers will be caught up in the clouds with Jesus.

Notable Verses:

2 Thessalonians 2:3 KJV
Let no man deceive you by any means: for that day shall not come, except there come a falling away first, and that man of sin be revealed, the son of perdition;

2 Thessalonians 3:6 KJV
Now we command you, brethren, in the name of our Lord Jesus Christ, that ye withdraw yourselves from every brother that walketh disorderly, and not after the tradition which he received of us.

CHAPTER 54: 1 TIMOTHY

This book is a letter that Paul wrote to the church around 62 AD and it was written to Timothy who was a young pastor at the time in Ephesus. The purpose of the letter was to encourage Timothy.

In the first chapter, we find that Paul is greeting Timothy and then he quickly begins focusing on false teaching and tells Timothy to fight the good fight.

In the next two chapters, Paul tells Timothy that God desires for all men to be saved. He also tells Timothy that there is only one God and the only way to him is through Jesus.

Paul also talks about some important guidelines for the leaders in the church, including women in the church, the deacons, and the overseer. He teaches that the church needs to focus on publicly reading the scripture and teaching.

Next, Paul discusses how relationships are to be handled in the church, how to discipline within the church and how to care for the widows. He lays down guidelines for those that are wealthy as well.

Notable Verses:

1 Timothy 4:1 KJV
Now the Spirit speaketh expressly, that in the latter times some shall depart from the faith, giving heed to seducing spirits, and doctrines of devils;
1 Timothy 3:5 KJV
For if a man know not how to rule his own house, how shall he take care of the church of God?

CHAPTER 55: 2 TIMOTHY

This book is a letter that was written by Paul to Timothy around 67 AD and many believe that this is that last letter that Paul wrote. Paul had been released from prison the first time around 62 AD but was imprisoned by Nero around 66 AD or 67 AD.

The purpose of this writing was to urge him to visit Paul one final time as well as to give him direction. The letter is somber and it is evident that Paul knew that his work had come to an end, his life on this Earth was done.

In the first two chapters, Paul starts off by telling Timothy to be strong and faithful, to join him in the suffering for the Gospel. He shows that it is his desire to ensure the saints have the knowledge that they need so that they are able to teach others.

In the next two chapters, Paul tells Timothy that difficult times are coming stating that men and women would become as they were in the times of Moses. In chapter four, Paul asks that some of his items be brought to him. It is believed that soon after this letter was written, most likely the spring of 68 AD, Paul was to be beheaded.

Notable Verses:

2 Timothy 4:7-8 KJV
7 I have fought the good fight, I have finished the race, I have kept the faith. 8 Now there is in store for me the crown of righteousness, which the Lord, the righteous Judge, will award to me on that day – and not only to me but also to all who have longed for his appearing.

2 Timothy 4:3 KJV

For the time will come when they will not endure sound doctrine; but after their own lusts shall they heap to themselves teachers, having itching ears;

CHAPTER 56: TITUS

The book of Titus is a letter that Paul wrote to Titus around 66 AD. The purpose of this writing was to guide Titus who was a Greek believer as he led the churches on Crete.

Paul writes this letter to encourage the young pastor when it comes to dealing with false teaching as well as the sinfulness of men.

In the first chapter, Paul tells Titus how he should choose leaders for the church and warns of those that are rebellious and deceivers.

In the second and third chapter, Paul teaches Titus how the believers of Christ should live healthy not only inside of the church but outside as well. He tells Titus to prepare for the coming of Christ and talks about how Jesus has saved us from our sins. He also states that when a believer dies, they go to be with Jesus.

Notable Verses:

Titus 3:5 KJV
Not by works of righteousness which we have done, but according to his mercy he saved us, by the washing of regeneration, and renewing of the Holy Ghost.
Titus 1:6 KJV
If any be blameless, the husband of one wife, having faithful children not accused of riot or unruly.

CHAPTER 57: PHILEMON

The book of Philemon is a letter that was written by Paul while he was in prison around 61 AD, to Philemon, asking for forgiveness for Onesimus, who was a servant of Philemon's who had run away. Onesimus was also a new believer. This book is only one-chapter long.

In the first seven verses, Paul greets Philemon, who was likely a member of the Colosse church and very wealthy. As we read, we can see that Paul is softening Philemon up before mentioning his servant that had run away.

In verses eight through twenty-five, we see that Paul appeals to Philemon on behave of Onesimus, who had met Paul in Rome after running away. It was then that Onesimus had turned his life over to God, however, under the Roman law, Philemon could have had the servant executed for running away.

Onesimus was the one that would deliver the letter to Philemon and is mentioned in a later letter, as a faithful brother.

Notable Verses:

Philemon 1:21 KJV
Having confidence in thy obedience I wrote unto thee, knowing that thou wilt also do more than I say.
Philemon 1:7 KJV
For we have great joy and consolation in thy love, because the bowels of the saints are refreshed by thee, brother.

CHAPTER 58: HEBREWS

The book of Hebrews was written to the Hebrew believers and it is unknown who the author is although many believe that it may have been Paul or Barnabas. The book was written to show that Jesus was superior to the old covenant or anything that the Law had to offer the people. It was written specifically for a group that was dealing with a lot of persecution at the time and considering returning to Judaism. The book was written around 67 AD.

In the first 10 chapters, we see the author telling the people repeatedly that Jesus is over everything, including the Old Testament. The author explains that a New Covenant has been made that is better than the old one because Jesus took on all of the sins of the people, being the last sacrifice.

In the next 9 chapters, the writer tells the people that faith is better than the work, which was what was required by the Old Covenant. He states that it is only through faith in Jesus that we are saved.

Notable Verses:

Hebrews 4:12 KJV
For the word of God is quick, and powerful, and sharper than any twoedged sword, piercing even to the dividing asunder of soul and spirit, and of the joints and marrow, and is a discerner of the thoughts and intents of the heart.

Hebrews 11:6 KJV

But without faith it is impossible to please him: for he that cometh to God must believe that he is, and that he is a rewarder of them that diligently seek him.

CHAPTER 59: JAMES

The book of James was written by the half-brother of Jesus, James around 48 or 49 AD. It is likely that this was actually the first letter included in the New Testament to ever be written. James wrote the book in order to encourage the Jewish believers to live Christian lives. It is about living a practical Christian life and being faithful. In many ways, James is quite similar to Proverbs.

In chapter one, James teaches that the believers need to test their faith and to take action as servants of Jesus. In the next two chapters we James talks about faith and works as well as the relationship between the two. He shows us that if a person has faith but no works, the faith is useless. It is a person's works that show that they have faith in Jesus. He teaches us that we are all sinners as well as if we break just one commandment we are guilty of breaking all of them.

In the last chapter he tells us that we have to submit ourselves to God and resist the devil, and in doing so, the devil will flee. The word prayer is used 7 times in this book, magnifying its importance in the life of a believer.

Notable Verses:

James 5:16 KJV
Confess your faults one to another, and pray one for another, that ye may be healed. The effectual fervent prayer of a righteous man availeth much.

James 5:13 KJV
Is any among you afflicted? let him pray. Is any merry? let him sing psalms.

CHAPTER 60: 1 PETER

This book is a letter that was written by Peter around 60 AD in order to encourage the Christians that were suffering at the time. The focus of this book is persecution.

In the first two chapters of this book, Peter tells the people to live a life of holiness, even when they are being persecuted. He teaches us that as Christians we should expect to suffer and be persecuted. He states that our salvation is secure because Christ took on our sins.

In the next two chapters of the book, Peter explains what it means to live a holy life and that part of it is obeying the commands of Jesus. He also states that Christians are also obligated to spread the gospel.

Notable Verses:

1 Peter 3:18 KJV
For Christ also hath once suffered for sins, the just for the unjust, that he might bring us to God, being put to death in the flesh, but quickened by the Spirit
1 Peter 1:3 KJV
Blessed be the God and Father of our Lord Jesus Christ, which according to his abundant mercy hath begotten us again unto a lively hope by the resurrection of Jesus Christ from the dead…

CHAPTER 62: 2 PETER

The second book of Peter is also a letter that was written by Peter around 63 AD and 64 AD. Peter wrote the letter in order to warn against the increase in number of false teachers.

In the first two chapters, Peter tells the church that the Gospel that they are teaching is of Jesus, giving them some reassurance. He talks about Gnosticism and how it was damaging the church. He tells the reader that God will judge the false prophets.

In the third chapter, Peter talks of the Day of the Lord as well as the new heaven and the new earth.

Notable Verses:

2 Peter 3:9 KJV
The Lord is not slack concerning his promise, as some men count slackness; but is longsuffering to us-ward, not willing that any should perish, but that all should come to repentance.

2 Peter 2:1 KJV
But there were false prophets also among the people, even as there shall be false teachers among you, who privily shall bring in damnable heresies, even denying the Lord that bought them, and bring upon themselves swift destruction.

CHAPTER 62: 1 JOHN

This book was a letter that was written by the Apostle John about 85 to 95 AD while in Ephesus. The purpose of this writing was to warn the readers about the increase of false teachers, who were denying that Jesus had actually come in a flesh body. It was the Gnostic view that John was writing about.

In the first two chapters, John tells the reader that God is light and in him, there is no darkness. He tells us that if our sins are confessed to Jesus, we would be cleansed of them. He also encourages the reader not to follow after the world stating that the world would pass away.

In the third and fourth chapters, John teaches about God's love and that it was because of his love for us that he sent Jesus to be a sacrifice.

In the last chapter, John tells us that we should live by faith and he shows us that he wants all believers to know that they will spend eternity with Jesus.

Notable Verses:

1 John 1:9 KJV
If we confess our sins, he is faithful and just to forgive us our sins, and to cleanse us from all unrighteousness.
1 John 4:1 KJV
Beloved, believe not every spirit, but try the spirits whether they are of God: because many false prophets are gone out into the world.

CHAPTER 63: 2 JOHN

The second book of John is a letter that was written by the Apostle John about 85 AD to 95 AD and it was written in order to ensure that the Christians did not lose their focus on Jesus as well as to warn about false prophets and teachings.

In the first three verses, John greets what is described as the chosen lady, whom many believe is one of the churches. In the next eight verses, which is the body of the letter, John tells us that we should love one another just as Jesus told us to. He also warns of antichrists and deceivers. He has to address the Gnosticism once again.

This book teaches us that those who do not follow and teach what Jesus taught are false teachers, antichrists that do not know Jesus.

Notable Verses:

2 John 1:5 KJV
And now I beseech thee, lady, not as though I wrote a new commandment unto thee, but that which we had from the beginning, that we love one another.
2 John 1:9 KJV
Whosoever transgresseth, and abideth not in the doctrine of Christ, hath not God. He that abideth in the doctrine of Christ, he hath both the Father and the Son.

CHAPTER 64: 3 JOHN

The third book of John is a letter that was written by the Apostle John between the years of 85 AD and 95 AD and it is the shortest book in the New Testament. The book was written to Gaius and Demetrius in order to praise them for their service.

In the first 12 verses, John gives praise to the teachers, then moves on to criticize Diotrephes who was a false teacher. John also speaks of another letter; which we do not have that he had sent to Diotrephes. However, Diotrephes had not accepted the letter and discouraged people from accepting those of the brethren church.

In the last few verses of the chapter, John states that he would rather visit them and talk face to face instead of writing.

Notable Verses:

3 John 1:3 KJV
For I rejoiced greatly when the brethren came and testified of the truth that is in thee, even as thou walkest in the truth.

3 John 1:10 KJV
Wherefore, if I come, I will remember his deeds which he doeth, prating against us with malicious words: and not content therewith, neither doth he himself receive the brethren, and forbiddeth them that would, and casteth them out of the church.

CHAPTER 65: JUDE

The book of Jude was written by the half-brother of Jesus, Jude and it was written around 75 AD. The purpose of this writing was to deal with the false teaching that had been going on and to illustrate the difference between those teachings and the teachings of Christ. The book of Jude is only one-chapter long.

In the first 16 verse, Jude begins talking about false teachings which were seeping into the Christian churches, causing disruptions and deception. In the next verses, Jude tells the Christians that they need to remember the words that were spoken by the apostles, referring to what had been taught about false prophets. He tells the people to focus on Christ and to watch that they are not misled.

Notable Verses:

Jude 1:5 KJV
I will therefore put you in remembrance, though ye once knew this, how that the Lord, having saved the people out of the land of Egypt, afterward destroyed them that believed not.

Jude 1:23 KJV
Now unto him that is able to keep you from falling, and to present you faultless before the presence of his glory with exceeding joy...

CHAPTER 66: REVELATION

The book of Revelation was written by the Apostle John who had not only followed Jesus but had witnessed his crucifixion. It was while John was on the Island of Patmos as a prisoner that he wrote the book around 85 AD to 95 AD. This book was written to provide encouragement for all who followed Christ as well as to warn of the judgment that would come in the last days on the nonbelievers. Revelation is a special book, as said by John, ""Blessed is he who reads and those who hear the words of the prophecy, and heed the things which are written in it; for the time is near."

In the first three chapters, John begins unveiling the truth. During this time, John was a prisoner on Patmos and he had received a vision. In this vision, he was told to write seven letters to the seven churches. In each letter, he talks about the churches as well as how they have failed and the qualities of each of them.

From chapters four through twenty John tells us what he had seen in his vision and when he speaks about Christ, he is called the Slain Lamb. It is this Lamb that is the only one that is able to open the seals. From here, we find that all except for the fifth seal bring judgment from God onto the earth. After the seven seals, we learn of the seven angels and the seven trumpets, each which bring judgment with them. It is at the point of the sixth trumpet that 1/3 of those in the Earth are killed.

Next, John sees a vision where he learns of the Antichrist and Satan. The seven angels are described as well as the seven bowls. Even after all of this, the people of the Earth do not repent and God rains down hail upon them.

We also learn about Hell, in this book, which is the Lake of Fire, where the Antichrist and the false prophet will be thrown into and where 1000 years later, the Devil himself will be thrown into. We learn that hell is a place of constant torment, night and day for all eternity.

In the last chapters of this book, we learn of the new heaven and the new Earth. We learn that it is Christ that will reign from the new Jerusalem and that it is only those whose names are found in the Lambs book of Life that will live with him forever.

Notable Verses:

Revelation 3:20 KJV
Behold, I stand at the door and knock: if any man hear my voice, and open the door, I will come in to him, and will sup with him, and he with me.
Revelation 21:1 KJV
And I saw a new heaven and a new earth: for the first heaven and the first earth were passed away; and there was no more sea.

LIKE THIS BOOK?

Check us out online or follow us on social media for exclusive deals and news on new releases!

 https://www.pinnaclepublish.com

 https://www.facebook.com/PinnaclePublishers/

 https://twitter.com/PinnaclePub

 https://www.instagram.com/pinnaclepublishers/

Made in the USA
Middletown, DE
16 April 2017